To Dye or Color Buttons:

To Prepare:

Lay several layers of newspaper on a flat working surface. Layer 3 - 4 paper towels. Use plastic spoons to remove items from dye solution.

Use only a heat-proof glass container, such as a canning jar or cup, to mix dye solution.

Buttons:

Tone down bright colors or blend many colors of buttons by dyeing them before beginning a necklace or project. White opaque plastic buttons dye most true to color; white pearl buttons dye well also.

Dye Solution:

Dissolve ½ teaspoon of Rit powder (or liquid) dye in ½ cup of boiling water in a heat-proof glass jar.

Test Dye Solution:

Place 3 or 4 buttons in the dye solution for 2 or 3 minutes. Remove and place on paper towels. If a deeper color is desired, return to dye for another 2 or 3 minutes. Some buttons take up to 15 minutes for desired color.

To speed coloring process, place glass container with dye and buttons in a microwave for 45 seconds. Once test buttons are the desired color, reheat dye solution and dye the remainder of buttons.

Place dyed buttons on paper towels to dry. Rinse buttons with cool water, place on clean paper towels to dry before using or wearing.

Adjust Shades:

If test buttons are too bright, add a few granules of Black dye to mute the color.

Colored buttons may be over-dyed to achieve a denser tone. For example, dye Red buttons Red or dye Green ones Green to achieve a richer and more uniform color.

Save Dye:

When you get the shade you want, save dye mixture until you complete the necklace.

You may need more buttons than recommended or you may wish to create matching earrings. If dye solution has cooled, place jar in a microwave for 45 seconds to reheat it.

Turquoise Flower Pin

The rich texture of wool gives this flower sophistication and style.
The button cluster in the center brings this flower life-like dimension.

SIZE: 5½" x 5½" - Use Pink patterns on page 12.

MATERIALS:

Wool or Felt fabric (Turquoise 5" x 5", Turquoise plaid 5" x 5", Mustard Yellow 4" x 4", Green plaid 3" x 6") • 15 assorted ½" buttons • Thread and needle • Sewing machine • Pin back 1¼"

INSTRUCTIONS:

Cut 2 large Turquoise flowers, 1 small Mustard flower, and 3 Green leaves.

Stitch Flower Petal & Leaf Folds: See instructions for Burgundy & Gold flower on page 4.

Assemble Flower: Place the Mustard Yellow flower on top of both Turquoise flowers. Stitch around the center circle ⅛" in from the bottom of petals and gather slightly. Sew buttons randomly into a cluster in the center of the flowers. Stitch leaves in place on the back. Stitch the pin back in place.

How to Make a Yo Yo:

Wonderful tools for making Yo-Yos and Pom Poms are made by **Clover Needlecraft.** These handy tools make construction easy.

1. Lay fabric on large part of a Yo Yo tool, snap it in place with 2nd part of the tool. Cut off excess fabric about ¼" from edge of tool.

2. Fold the edge under. Using doubled thread and a needle, sew an in and out Running stitch around the tool (thread should go 'into' the slots around rim of tool).

3. Remove the tool. Pull thread to gather the edge of fabric. This will form a Yo Yo. Make a few extra stitches across the opening. Tie off thread and hide the knot.

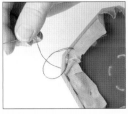

If you prefer to make Yo Yos and Pom Poms without a tool, it is also simple to do.

Yo Yos: Make Yo Yos by gathering along the edge of a fabric circle then pull up the gather as you tuck the ends inside. Tie a knot and take a few stitches

Pom Poms: Wrap fabric strips around cardboard. Pull a strip to tie the ball, then cut the loops.

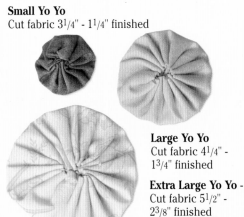

Small Yo Yo
Cut fabric 3¼" - 1¼" finished

Large Yo Yo
Cut fabric 4¼" - 1¾" finished

Extra Large Yo Yo -
Cut fabric 5½" - 2⅜" finished

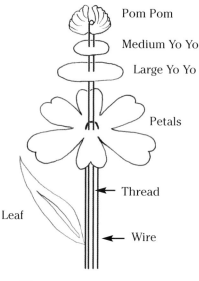

Pom Pom
Medium Yo Yo
Large Yo Yo
Petals
Thread
Leaf
Wire

Large Flower - 5" diameter

Cut 6" squares (2 fabric, 1 heavy iron-on interfacing). Sandwich the layers together then trace and cut out the petals shape. If desired, topstitch $1/4$" from the edges and in the center. Repeat to make 2 large leaves.

Cut 2 fabric circles ($5\frac{1}{2}$", $4\frac{1}{4}$") and make each into a Yo Yo.

Make a small ($1\frac{5}{8}$") Pom Pom (Use a Yellow Small Pom Pom tool or a 1" piece of cardboard) with $1/4$" strips of fabric.

Use doubled pearl cotton thread to sew UP through petals, both Yo Yos and the Pom Pom, then sew DOWN through the shapes. Reinforce petals with wire.

Align the thread and wire with a stem. Wrap with floral tape, adding 2 large leaves about 3" down.

Burgundy & Gold Flower Pin

Accessorize your outfits with sophistication with this flower pin. The beauty and body of the wool fabric make this flower both sturdy and gorgeous.

SIZE: 5" x 5" - Use Pink patterns on page 12

MATERIALS:

Wool or felt (Burgundy 5" x 10", Marigold 4" x 4", Green 3" x 6") • Print fabric circle $3\frac{1}{4}$" • Buttons (1", $3/8$", $1/4$") • Thread and needle • Sewing machine • Pin back $1\frac{1}{4}$"

INSTRUCTIONS:

Cut 2 large Burgundy flowers, 1 small Marigold flower, 3 Sage Green leaves.

Stitch Flower Petal & Leaf Folds: On each flower, fold each petal in half lengthwise. On the backside, stitch with a $1/8$" seam on the sewing machine from the bottom of petal where it meets the center to $1/4$" from the outside edge of petal.

Stitch the leaves in the same way with a $1/8$" seam starting at the bottom of each leaf to $1/2$" from the top of each leaf. Use an iron to press flower petals and leaves lightly so they will stay open, but do not flatten.

Assemble Flower: Put 1 Burgundy flower on top of the other placing the petals of the top flower in between the petals of the bottom flower. Put the Marigold flower on top of both Burgundy flowers. Sew a gathering stitch in a circle in the center $1/8$" from the bottom edge of the petals. Gather slightly so the petals stand up.

Cut a $3\frac{1}{4}$" circle from print fabric. Make a fabric Yo Yo. Place Yo Yo in the center of the flower.

Layer the buttons. Stitch in place. Stitch the leaves in place on the back. Stitch pin back in place.

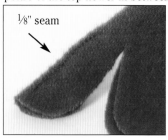

$1/8$" seam

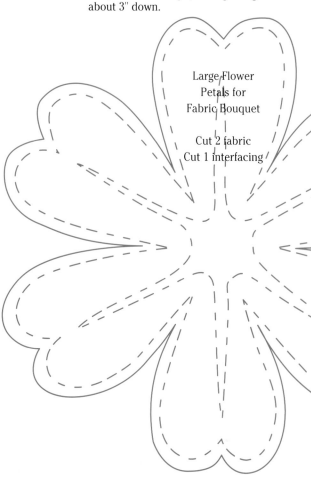

Large Flower Petals for Fabric Bouquet

Cut 2 fabric
Cut 1 interfacing

Fabric Bouquet

Create a gorgeous bouquet that will never fade and no one will be allergic to the pollen! Use scraps from your fabric stash for this fun project.

SIZE: Small blooms 3" • Large Petal flowers 5" diameter • Leaf clusters 6"

MATERIALS:
Fabrics • Heavy iron-on interfacing • Pearl cotton thread • 22 Chenille needle • Floral stem wire • Green florist tape • Green paddle wire • Pinking shears • Buttons (¾", ⅜", ¼")

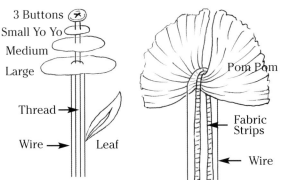

Small Blooms - 3" diameter

Cut 3 fabric circles (5½", 4¼" x 3¼") and make each circle into a Yo Yo.

Use doubled pearl cotton thread to sew UP through Yo Yos and 3 buttons, then sew DOWN through the shapes. Reinforce petals with wire. Align the thread and wire with a stem. Wrap with floral tape, adding 2 small leaves.

Leaf Clusters - 4½" diameter

Make a large (4½") Pom Pom with ¼" strips of fabric. (Use a Turquoise X-large Pom Pom tool or a 2½" piece of cardboard). Reinforce Pom Pom with wire.

Align the fabric strips and wire with a stem. Wrap with floral tape.

Large Leaf
for
Fabric Bouquet

Cut 2 fabric
Cut 1 interfacing

Small
Leaf for
Fabric Bouquet

Cut 2 fabric
Cut 1 interfacing

Refer to a book on Crochet for stitches
Stitches Used: Chain (ch)
Single crochet (sc)
Double crochet (dc)
Slip stitch (sl st)
Treble (tr)
Gauge: 8 sc = 1"

INSTRUCTIONS:
Ch 200.

Row 1: Sc in 2nd chain from hook and in each of the next 48 ch. Work (ch 1, skip next ch, sc in next ch) 52 times. Sc in each chain to end. Ch 7 for closure loop. Turn.

Row 2: Sc in each sc to first chain-1 loop. *For shell, work 5 dc in chain-1 loop, sc in next chain-1 loop. Repeat from * to make 26 shells. Sc in each sc to end, sc in turning chain.

Fasten off. Weave in ends.

Sew ½" button to band end for closure.

Row 3: With right side facing, attach thread with sl st in 2nd dc of last shell made. Sc in center dc of shell. *For fan, work 7 tr in next sc between shells. Sc in center dc of next shell. Ch 3, sc in center dc of next shell.

Repeat from * 11 times. Work 7 tr in next sc between last 2 shells - 13 fans. Sc in center dc of last shell. Sc in next dc. Ch 1, turn.

Row 4: NOTE: Attach buttons in size and color order as desired with chain loops. For each loop, ch 1, 3 or 5, attach button through 1 hole, then make the same number of chains above button.

For better balance, attach smaller buttons with shorter chain loops, attach larger buttons with longer chain loops. Sc in next sc, ch 1, sc in one hole of button to attach, ch 1, sc in same sc.

Work (sc in next tr, ch, attach button, ch, sc in same tr). *Sc in sc at tip of shell, ch, attach button, ch, sc in chain-3 loop. Sc in chain-3 loop, sc in shank of ¾" button, sc in chain-3 loop. Sc in sc at tip of next shell, ch 1, attach button, ch, sc in next tr.

Work (sc in next tr, ch, attach button, ch, sc in next tr) around next fan. Repeat from * across. Alternate ½" shank buttons with ¾" shank buttons in chain-3 loops.

To end, sc in sc at tip of last shell, attach button with chain-1 loop, sc in next stitch of shell. Fasten off. Weave in ends.

Rainbow of Buttons Necklace

Catch a rainbow of sunny colors! Wearing this cheerful necklace will lift your spirits and brighten your day.

SIZE: 33"

MATERIALS:
117 assorted buttons including 6 matching ¾" shank, 6 matching ½" shank, one ½" for closure
• Size 8 crochet hook • Size 10 cotton crochet thread

INSTRUCTIONS:

Ch 44.

Row 1: Work 4 dc in 4th chain from hook for first shell. *Ch 4, shell in 4th chain from hook. Repeat from * 13 times - 15 shells. Ch 41, turn.

Row 2: Sc in 2nd chain from hook and in each of the next 40 chains. *Work (dc, ch 1) 6 times in chain-4 loop at side of shell, dc in loop, ch 3 for first fan. Sc in top of chain-4 loop of next shell.

Repeat from * 6 times. Work (dc, ch 1) 7 times in chain-4 loop of last shell - 8 fans. Skip 1 chain of foundation chain, sc in each chain to end.

Ch 7 for closure loop, turn.

Row 3: Sc in each of the next 3 sc, work (ch 3, sl st in 3rd chain from hook) for picot. *Sc in each of the next 3 sc, picot.

Repeat from * 10 times - 12 picots. Sc in each sc to fan, sc in each chain-1 loop and dc of fan. *Ch 3, sc in each dc and chain-1 loop around next fan. Repeat from * across fans - 104 sc, 7 chain-3 loops. Work (sc in each of the next 3 sc, picot) 12 times. Sc in each sc to end, sc in turning chain.

Fasten off. Weave in ends. Sew a ½" button to center of band end for closure.

Row 4: Attach buttons around bottom of fans as follows:

With right side facing, attach thread with sl st in last sc of band before last fan made. Work (sc in first sc on fan, ch 1 loosely, sc in one hole of ½" button, ch 1 loosely, sc in next sc of fan. Sc in next sc, ch 3, attach ⅞" button, ch 3, sc in next sc. Sc in next sc, ch 5, attach ⅞" button, ch 5, sc in next sc. *Sc in next sc, ch 3, attach ½" button, ch 3, sc in next sc. Sc in next sc, ch 5, attach ⅞" button, ch 5, sc in next sc. Sc in next sc, ch 7, attach ⅞" button, ch 7, sc in next sc. Sc in next sc, ch 9, attach 1" button, ch 9, sc in chain-3 loop. Sc in next sc, attach 1" button with chain-9 loop, sc in next sc.

Continue in the same manner to attach buttons as follows: Chain-7 loop with 1" button, chain-5 loop with ⅞" button, chain-3 loop with ½" button, chain-5 loop with ⅞" button, chain-7 loop with 1" button, chain-9 loop with 1" button, sc in chain-3 loop. ** Sc in next sc, attach 1" button with chain-7 loop, sc in next sc. Sc in next sc, attach ⅞" button with chain-5 loop, sc in next sc. Sc in next sc, attach ⅞" button with chain-5 loop.

Repeat * to ** to center chain-3 loop. Sc in same chain-3 then repeat (to) in reverse order to create a mirror image of first side.

To end, join with sl st in first sc of band. Fasten off. Weave in ends.

Button Dangles Necklace

Gorgeous earth tones complement every item in your wardrobe. Wonderful to wear with your favorite silk blouse, this necklace is lovely with skirts and jeans.

SIZE: 22"

MATERIALS:
Brown buttons (eleven ½", twenty-four ⅞", twenty-two 1")
• Size 8 crochet hook • Size 10 cotton crochet thread

Button Jewelry

Buttons take on a new charm when used to make these beautiful bracelets.

They can be elegant, whimsical, or casual, depending on how you put them together. Try different colors and sizes for a whole new look.

Ruby Red and Pearls Bracelet

This bracelet is great for casual wear and can easily be adapted to any color scheme of your favorite color.

SIZE: 8½"
MATERIALS:
Buttons (12 Red ⅝" 4-hole, 12 White ⁷⁄₁₆" pearl, 12 Red ⁵⁄₁₆") • 1 yard of Black 1mm leather jewelry cord • Masking tape

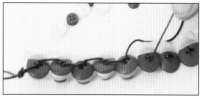

INSTRUCTIONS:
Place top of Red ⅝" buttons on masking tape so holes are in a horizontal line and are not covered by tape. Buttons should almost touch. Pass cord DOWN in left hole of first button. On same button, bring cord back UP through hole directly across.

Leave 4" of cord sticking out on left side of first button. The long piece will be used for threading.

Repeat this threading in each of 11 buttons. Fold cord so a 1½" loop sticks out. Tie a knot, leaving a ½" loop for a closure, but do not cut the cord.

Thread cord UP through one hole that does not have cord in it. Thread on a White button and a small Red button, then take cord back DOWN through all 3 buttons in hole across from the one you came up. On backside of bracelet, thread cord UP. Thread will alternate as you continue.

Continue threading on buttons all the way across, keeping the cord tight as you go. Tie the cord ends in a small knot close to buttons. Make a knot for closure. Clip the ends of the cord and carefully remove masking tape.

Spring Fling Circles Bracelet

Spring flowers made of buttons add a whimsical touch to this adorable bracelet.

SIZE: 9"
TIP: To alter length, change the size of buttons and adjust felt circles. Adjust ribbon length before attaching clasps.
Button sizes: large ¾" medium, ½", small ⅜"
MATERIALS:
Buttons: Mint Green (1, 12, 1), Lavender (1, 6, 2), Pink (1, 6, 2), Blue (2, 6, 1) • ⅝" wide ribbon clamps • 1" lobster clasp • 9 Silver ³⁄₁₆" jump rings • 7½" of Pink ⅝" grosgrain ribbon • White felt 2" x 7" • Thread and needle • Flat-nose pliers
INSTRUCTIONS:
Cut 5 felt 1½" circles. Sew 6 medium buttons around edge of each circle. Sew a large button to center on top of the inside edges of buttons. Sew a small button in the center of each.

Center a flower on Pink ribbon leaving ½" of ribbon sticking out on one side. Stitch in place. Sew remaining flowers.
TIP: Overlap edges of felt as needed to achieve correct length.

Trim ribbon ½" from edge of felt. Use pliers to close clamps on ends of ribbon. Attach clasp with a jump ring. On the other end, attach 5 jump rings and a small Pink button.

Colorful Stacked Button Bracelet

Intense purple, burgundy, and ripe citrus colors capture the zest of harvest time. This charming bracelet is a beautiful addition to any fall wardrobe. The gold beads give this bracelet a warm seasonal glow.

SIZE: 8"
Tip: This makes a 7" bracelet that is adjustable to 8". To change the length, alter the size of buttons or change the number of sets.
MATERIALS:
15 autumn color ¾" buttons • 14mm Gold lobster clasp • 9 Gold ³⁄₁₆" jump rings • 1 Gold heart charm • 7 Gold 5mm beads • 2 Gold 4mm knot covers • *DMC* pearl cotton • Masking tape • Flat-nose pliers • Needle with a small eye • Super glue

INSTRUCTIONS:
Cut 45" of thread. Tie a large knot in one end. Apply a dot of glue over knot to secure. Use a needle to thread a knot cover onto thread and over the knot. Be sure knot cover is threaded so the ring on it is sticking out away from thread. Close knot cover over the knot with flat-nose pliers.

For bottom row of buttons, place top of each button onto tape, making sure tape does not cover any buttonholes. Adhere buttons slightly touching. Fold excess tape onto itself, but not over the buttons. Using first button from bottom row. Take threaded needle UP through one buttonhole, then go DOWN in hole across from it. You want the knot cover to stick out from the side of this first button with as little thread showing as possible.
TIP: Button with 4 holes, come UP in an empty hole, go DOWN in the hole across.
TIP: Button with 2 holes, go through both holes again. This will stabilize buttons.

Repeat threading process for next 7 buttons. Now take thread back through buttons going UP and DOWN in the holes in a horizontal line to get the thread back to first button. Come up through hole of closest button.

Bring thread UP through one hole and back DOWN through the hole across on the first button. Now take thread through second button on bottom row in the hole closest to first button. Go back UP through same holes, then thread on a Gold bead. Go DOWN through the same holes. Repeat with next 6 buttons.

Once the last button is in place, go through two holes on last bottom layer button to secure thread. Thread on second knot cover, tie a large knot in thread so knot is just to the outside of last button. Cut the thread and close knot cover as before.

Attach 7 jump rings to one side of bracelet to make bracelet extension chain. Use 8th jump ring to attach a heart charm. On other side use a jump ring to attach clasp to knot cover. Remove tape from the back of buttons.

Blue Bliss Bracelet

The varying blue tones in this bracelet will look great with jeans and be an addition to your casual attire.

SIZE: 7"
Tip: Alter length of this bracelet by adding/subtracting buttons in each set of the pattern. Measure before tying cords to ensure that you have the desired length.
MATERIALS:
24" of .5mm stretch bead & jewelry cord • 6 Silver 6mm beads • Blue buttons (twenty-four ¼", twelve ⅜", twelve ½", six ¾") • E6000 glue

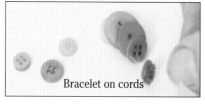
Bracelet on cords

Earrings on head pins

INSTRUCTIONS:
Cut cording into two 12" pieces. Place one end of each cord inside the fold of a folded piece of tape. To string buttons, place cords through opposite holes in the same button. String buttons in this pattern:
2 – ¼" • 1 – ⅜" • 1 – ½" • 1 – ¾" • 1 – ½" • 1 – ⅜" • 2 – ¼" • 1 Silver bead

Repeat this pattern 6 times. Take one end of taped cord out of tape and tie it in a knot with other end of that cord. Take other end of taped cord out of tape and tie it in a knot with other end of that cord. Secure knots with glue. Let dry overnight. Trim cord.

Black Velvet Band

Step out in style with an elegant velvet bracelet.

SIZE: 7½"

TIP: Alter length of ribbon before attaching clamps.

MATERIALS:
Ribbon (5½" of ⅞" Black velvet, 13" of 1½" Ivory grosgrain, 11" of ⅞" Black satin) • 25 Ivory 4mm pearl beads • 7 buttons ⅜" (Clear, Ivory, or Cream) • 1" Silver ⅛" wide chain • 2 Silver ⅞" wide ribbon clamps • 4 Silver 6mm split rings • 1 Antique Silver heart toggle clasp • Black acrylic paint • Clear acrylic matte coating • Thread and Beading needle • Pliers (Flat-nose, Split ring) • Wire cutters

INSTRUCTIONS:

Smear Black paint over Silver clamps. Push paint into grooves, gently wipe away excess to antique them. Let dry. Spray with 2-3 coats of Clear acrylic. Let dry.

Sew ends of ribbons together along width. Gather long edges to make an Ivory and a Black circle. Position on bracelet.

Clamp ends on Black velvet ribbon. With wire cutters, cut off 2 links of chain and attach to heart with a split ring. Attach chain to a clamp. Cut 5 links of chain, attach to other toggle closure with a split ring. Attach this chain to second clamp with a split ring.

Sew gathered circles in the center of Black ribbon. Sew buttons and pearls in place.

Yo Yo Ornaments

Little Yo Yos turn fabrics into cute holiday decorations for a wall, window or holiday tree.

MATERIALS:
(to make 1 of each design)
Fabric:
⅓ yd Green, ⅛ yd White,
¼ yd Red,
4" x 4" Black, 4" x 4" Yellow
Buttons:
1 Gold snowflake ¾", 3 Green ½"
Black: one ⅞", one ½"
Red: twenty-seven ½", one ¾"
10" Red ⅜" wide ribbon
DMC Red embroidery floss
Sewing thread and needle
22 Chenille needle

INSTRUCTIONS:
Cut 4" circles for Yo Yos:
    22 Green, 5 Red, 1 Yellow,
    5 White, 1 Black.
Cut a 5" Red circle and
    a 6" Red circle for the flower.
Make all circles into Yo Yos.

Wreath

SIZE: Wreath: 4½" x 4½"
    Sew 9 Yo Yos in a circle. Shape the ribbon into a bow and sew to the top Yo Yo. Sew the large Red button over the ribbon. Sew a small Red button over the opening of remaining Yo Yos.

Candy Cane

SIZE: Candy Cane 3½" x 5½"
    Position the following Yo Yos in a candy cane shape: Red-White-Red-White-Red-White-Red-White-Red. Tack the Yo Yos together. Sew a Red button on each Yo Yo.

Flower

SIZE: Flower: 4" x 4½"
    Stack a small White Yo Yo and medium Red Yo Yo on a large Red Yo Yo. Tack together. Sew a large Black button on top. Tack 3 Green Yo Yos to outer edge of large Red flower base. Sew a button to each Green Yo Yo.

Tree:

SIZE: Tree: 4½" x 6"
    Sew a base row of 4 Green Yo Yos together. Sew the next row with 3 Yo Yos, followed by 2, then 1. Tack the rows together to form the tree. Sew a Red button to each Green Yo Yo. Sew the snowflake button to the Yellow Yo Yo and tack to the top of the tree. Sew a Black button to the Black Yo Yo and tack to the bottom of the tree.

Ribbon Tag Fob

MATERIALS:
Buttons (¼" Black, 2 White ¾" flowers, 5 Pink ½") • 1 Silver swivel hook for a ⅞" strap • Ribbon (6½" grosgrain 1½" wide, 18" Hot Pink ⁷⁄₁₆" wide) • 3½" Hot Pink eye-lash trim • 6" iron-on adhesive hem tape ¾" wide • Sewing thread • Sewing needle • Iron

INSTRUCTIONS:
    Cut hem tape into two 3" pieces. Pass printed ribbon through the bottom of the hook and fold so the ends meet. Place 2 strips of hem tape between the ribbon and iron together.
    Sew the Black buttons to the ribbon to form a letter.
    Wrap the eyelash trim around the bottom of the ribbon and sew in place. Sew flower buttons in place.
    Sew the Pink buttons along the bottom covering parts of the Pink trim. Tie Pink ribbon around the hook.

Key Ring Fob

MATERIALS:
Buttons (1 Red heart, 10 assorted ¼", 4 assorted ⅝") • 1 Silver square key ring • Silver 6mm split rings • Silver jump rings (6mm, 9mm) • 5" Silver chain ⅛" wide • Pliers (Split ring, Flat-nose) • Wire cutters

INSTRUCTIONS:
    Cut 2" of chain. Then cut 6 pieces of 4 chain links. Use a split ring to attach the 2" chain to the key ring.
    Attach the Red heart to the end of the 2" chain with a 9mm jump ring. Use jump rings to attach buttons to the small pieces of chain.
    Attach small chains with split rings.

Cell Phone or Flash Drive Fob

MATERIALS:
1 lanyard • 7 jump rings 9mm • 7 Lavender ½" buttons • Flat-nose pliers

INSTRUCTIONS:
    Attach buttons to one another in groups of 2 or 3 with jump rings.
    Use a jump ring to attach to the cell phone lanyard.

Pencil Fob

MATERIALS:
Buttons (2 Blue ⁷⁄₁₆", 2 White ⁷⁄₁₆", 3 Red ⁵⁄₁₆") • 2 Silver 4mm beads • 2 jump rings 6mm • 6mm split ring • #6 Plumbing O-ring ⁷⁄₁₆" outer diameter x ¹⁄₁₆" • 12" Black 1mm jewelry cord • Jewelry pliers

INSTRUCTIONS:
    Thread the buttons onto the Black cord: Red, Blue, White, Red, Blue, White, Red. Thread the split ring onto the cord. Thread the cord back through the buttons using a different hole. Tie a knot.
    Thread a Silver bead onto each end of the cord, tie a knot and trim.
    Attach a jump ring to the plumbing O-ring. Use the second jump ring to attach split ring to the first jump ring.
    Thread a pencil through the O ring.

Fabulous Fobs

If you're looking for a way to dress up some of the ordinary things in your life, then these fobs are for you.

Whether it's your purse, your cell phone, a backpack, or a zipper, these projects will encourage you to display your sense of style and creativity on everything.

MANY THANKS to my staff for their cheerful help and wonderful ideas!

Kathy Mason
Patty Williams
Donna Kinsey
Kristy Krouse
David & Donna Thomason

Paula Phillips

Paula is an innovative designer who loves all types of crafting. She has been designing for over a decade and her designs have appeared in many books.

She teaches classes and is a digital designer. View more of her work at paulaphillips.blogspot.com.

Key Ring Fob

Attach buttons to one another in groups of 2 or 3 with jump rings and round-nose jewelry pliers.

Use a jump ring to attach the cluster of buttons to a chain.

Blue Flower Pin

Wintry blues, icy crystals, and snow white pearls combine in a flower pin guaranteed to brighten the lapel of any jacket. It will also look great on a handbag or backpack.

SIZE: 4" x 4" - Use Lavender and Blue patterns

MATERIALS:
Wool or Felt fabric (Denim Blue, Baby Blue, Lavender print) • 5 Buttons ($\frac{3}{4}$", $\frac{3}{8}$", $\frac{1}{4}$") • 6 Blue E-beads • 3" of pearls on a string • 3" Lavender $\frac{3}{8}$" wide ribbon • Thread and needle • Pin back 1$\frac{1}{4}$"

INSTRUCTIONS:
Cut large and small flowers from Denim felt. Cut medium flower from printed felt. Cut 8 small petals from Baby Blue felt.

With a needle and thread, fold one of the Baby Blue petals in half lengthwise and $\frac{3}{16}$" up from the bottom of the petal, run the thread through the petal just inside the edge. Then bring the thread back over the top and run through the same way, just $\frac{1}{16}$" up from the first stitch. Pull tight to gather the petal.

On the same thread, repeat this with the other 7 petals to form a flower. Stitch the last petal to first petal and tie a knot.

Place Baby Blue flower on top of Lavender and Denim flowers. Stitch in the center. Fold Lavender ribbon, stitch in place. Repeat for pearl string. Place small Blue flower on top, stitch in place.

Randomly stitch buttons and beads. Sew the pin back.

Blue Flower Pin
Small Flower Cut 1
Lavender

Blue Flower
Small Petals
Cut 8 Baby Blue

Turquoise or
Burgundy Flowers
Leaf
(pages 3 - 4)

Cut 3 Green

Blue Flower Pin
Small Flower
Cut 1 Denim Blue

Blue Flower Pin
Large Flower

Cut 1 Denim Blue

Turquoise or
Burgundy Flowers
(pages 3 - 4)
Large Petals

Cut 1

Turquoise or
Burgundy Flowers
(pages 3 - 4)
Small Petals
Cut 1

Fluffy Button Tee

Sew seeds of love into center of this adorable shirt. Kids will love the bright colors and texture of this design.

SIZE: 8" diameter

MATERIALS:
1 Lime Green T-shirt • Fleece (⅛ yard bright print, ⅛ yard Yellow) • 35 bright assorted buttons (⅝" - ½" - ⅜")

INSTRUCTIONS:
Cut 6 pieces of fleece 3½" x 4". Sew a gathering stitch along a 4" side of each piece. Position on shirt, pin in place.

Cut a Yellow fleece 3¾" circle. Place a small handful of stuffing into the open center of petals. Place circle over the edges of the petals and stuffing and pin in place.

Stitch along outside of circle with a ⅜" seam. Sew petals in place at the top on each side. Sew buttons in the center of Yellow circle.

Cheerful T-Shirts

Catch a rainbow of sunny colors with these button embellished shirts! Kids will love the bright colors and the texture of these designs. Any child wearing these cheerful shirts will lift your spirits and brighten your day.

Be sure to embroider the details instead of using buttons when the shirt will be worn by a baby, toddler or young child.

BASIC MATERIALS:
T-shirt • Fleece for applique • Polyfil stuffing • Assorted buttons • Pinking shears • Thread and needle • Sewing machine

Pink
Cheeks
Cut 2

Sunshine Applique

It's a sunshine smiling shirt! Brighten your day with this happy T-shirt. Pearlescent buttons circling the face make this sun radiant.

SIZE: 7½" diameter

MATERIALS:
1 White T-shirt • Fleece (⅛ yd Yellow, 2" x 2" Pink) • Buttons (2 Black ½", 21 Pearlescent ⅜") • *DMC* embroidery floss (Black)

INSTRUCTIONS:
Cut a 3¾" circle and 8 triangles from Yellow fleece. Using regular scissors, cut two ¾" circles from Pink fleece. Embroider a mouth onto the large circle with a Running stitch and Black floss.

Sew Pink circles and 2 Black buttons to the face. Set aside. Place triangle pieces on T-shirt to form sunrays and pin in place. Make sure the large circle will cover the inside edges of sunrays.

Sew triangles onto the shirt.
Sew the large circle in place leaving an opening for stuffing.
Stuff, then stitch opening closed.
Sew 21 buttons around the face.

Sunshine
Yellow
Triangles
Cut 8

Friendship Cards

Buttons make fun and beautiful decorations on cards.

They can be stamped and colored, sewn on, glued on and used in many ways to add adorable embellishment and dimension.

Enjoy the Moments

Make someone's day by sending them this terrific card. The button frame stitched with love lets them know how much you care.

SIZE: 4¼" x 5½"

MATERIALS:
Ivory card 4¼" x 5½" • Decorative papers (Leaf print, Sage Green, Ivory) • 18" Sage Green ribbon ⅛" wide • Word stamp • Burgundy inkpad • Sewing needle • Thread • Tape runner • Glue dots

INSTRUCTIONS:
Ink the edges of leaf paper. Wrap ribbon around the bottom. Adhere leaf paper to card. • Stamp the word image on Ivory paper. Layer Ivory paper onto Sage Green paper.

Stitch buttons randomly along the inside edge of the Sage Green paper. Adhere to card.

Tie a ribbon bow and adhere to card.

Butterfly 'Thinking of You'

Let your friends and family know how much you care with this precious card. The scalloped edges give this card a sweet softness that will make anyone feel special.

SIZE: 4" x 5½"

MATERIALS:
White card 4" x 5½" • Decorative papers (Mint Green, Print, Yellow) • Buttons (2 Mint Green ⁷⁄₁₆", 5 Dark Pink ⁵⁄₁₆", 1 Dark Pink ½") • Mint Green marker • Inkpads (Mint Green, Dark Pink, Yellow) • Rubber stamps (Small flower, "Thinking of you") • Scallop paper edge scissors • Glue dots • Tape runner

INSTRUCTIONS:
Adhere layered papers across the bottom of card. Stamp words. Adhere Green buttons.

Trace the large butterfly pattern onto the backside of the Mint Green paper and cut out using the scallop edge scissors. Trace the smaller butterfly pattern onto the back of the print paper and cut out with regular scissors. Ink the edges. Trace the inside wing patterns onto the back of the Yellow paper and cut out. Ink the edges. Adhere the butterfly to the card.

Adhere five ⁵⁄₁₆" Pink buttons to the center of body. Glue the ½" Pink button at the top.

Draw the antennae with the Mint Green marker. Stamp small flowers at the end of each antenna. Ink the edges of the front of the card.

Dragonfly Buttons Card

Stamping designs on buttons is a great way to embellish cards. This card features a dragonfly stamped on three buttons to make an adorable invitation.

SIZE: 4" x 5½"

MATERIALS:
White card 4" x 5½" • 3 Ivory 2-hole ⅞" flat buttons • Decorative paper (Lavender, Purple) • Rubber stamps (Dragonfly, Words: "Caring", "Sharing", "fun!") • Purple embroidery floss • Tsukineko StazOn Black inkpad • Purple inkpad • Permanent markers (Purple, Yellow) • Clear acrylic matte spray sealer • Adhesive

INSTRUCTIONS:
Stamp a dragonfly on each button with StazOn ink. Let dry.

Color dragonflies with markers. let dry. Spray with 2 light coats of the Clear acrylic sealer.

Layer squares onto paper strip. Sew buttons in place. Adhere cardstock and stamped words to card.

Adhere button strip to card.

Doll Card

Make someone smile. Perfect for any little girl and everyone who loves dolls, this all occasion card is sure to please.

SIZE: 4" x 5½"

MATERIALS:
White card 4" x 5½" • Ivory Buttons (6 - ⅜", 4 - ⁷⁄₁₆", one 2-hole 1⁵⁄₁₆" button for face) • Decorative papers (Light Blue, Royal Blue) • 1½" x 3" Blue print fabric • 2 yds Tan yarn or floss • 1 yd Blue ⅛" wide grosgrain ribbon • Black permanent pen • Tsukineko Pink StazOn inkpad • Cotton swab • ¼" x 4" cardboard • Pinking shears • Thread and needle • Glue dots • Tape runner • Fabric glue • Double-sided adhesive tape

INSTRUCTIONS:
Adhere Light Blue paper and ribbon to card. Using the pattern, cut the dress out of the Royal Blue paper. Cut around the edges of the fabric skirt with pinking shears. Sew a gathering stitch along the top of the 3" width of the fabric and gather to 1" across. Adhere the fabric skirt to the dress. Cut 10" of ribbon and tie into a bow. Adhere to the skirt. Adhere dress to the card. Glue two ⅜" buttons for each leg, one ⁷⁄₁₆" button for each foot, one ⅜" button for each arm, and one ⁷⁄₁₆" button for each hand.

On the 1⁵⁄₁₆" button, draw a mouth with a permanent pen. To make the cheeks, dab the cotton swab on the Pink StazOn inkpad and lightly dab the ink onto the button where the cheeks should be. Use the dry end of the cotton swab in a circular motion to blend the ink into the button. Adhere the button face to the card.

To make hair, cut ten 5" lengths of yarn. Place a 5" base yarn along the length of cardboard. Wrap 5" yarn around cardboard and the 5" piece of base yarn. Wrap it 6 times, then cut the long piece of yarn. Use 5" piece of base yarn to pull wrapped pieces tightly together, then tie 5" base yarn into a knot.

Trim ends that are not in a loop ¼" from the knot. These ends will become the doll's bangs. Repeat this process to make 4 more hair pieces, but for the last 4, only wrap 4 times, and trim very close to the knot. Glue hair in place.

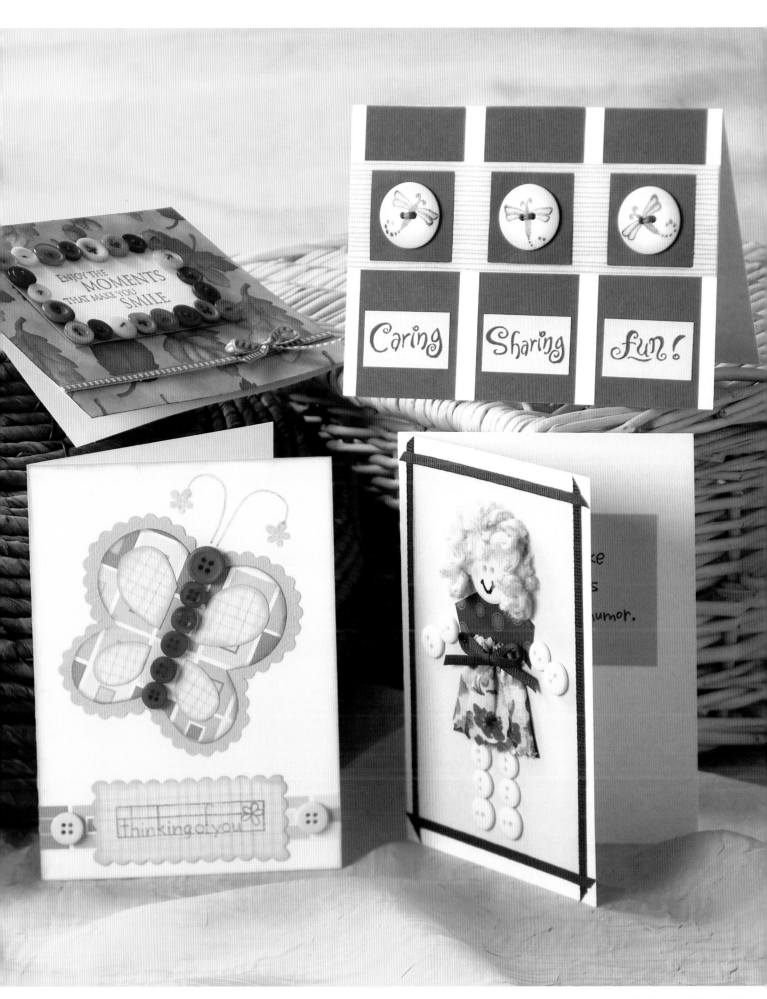

ENJOY THE
MOMENTS
THAT MAKE YOU
SMILE

Caring   Sharing   fun!

thinking of you

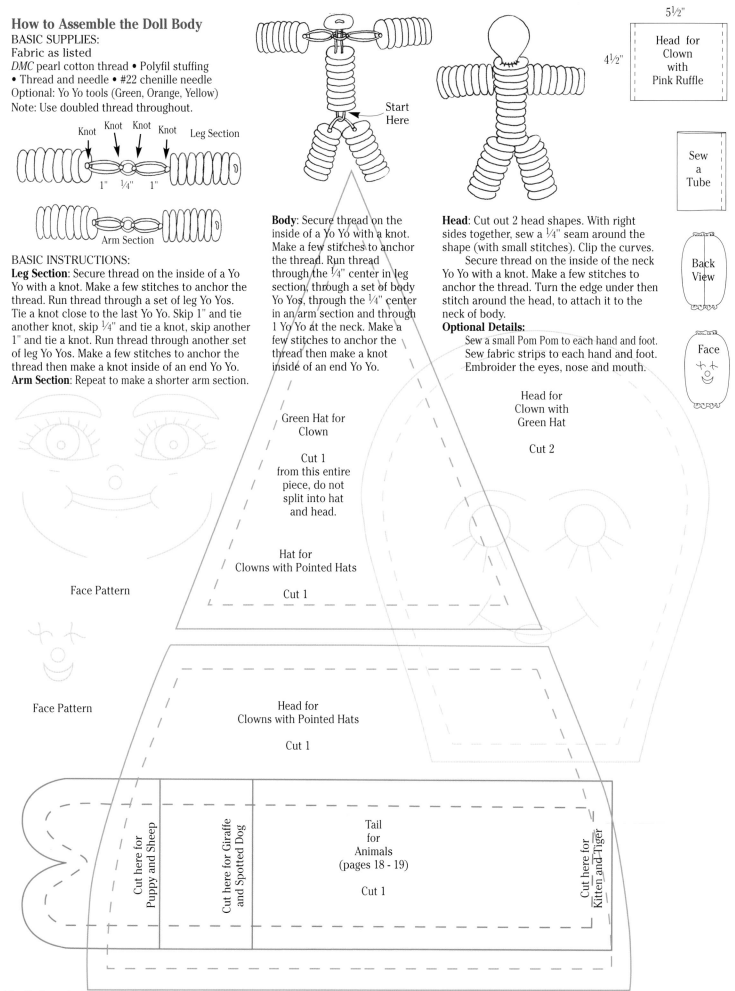

How to Assemble the Doll Body

BASIC SUPPLIES:
Fabric as listed
DMC pearl cotton thread • Polyfil stuffing
• Thread and needle • #22 chenille needle
Optional: Yo Yo tools (Green, Orange, Yellow)
Note: Use doubled thread throughout.

Knot   Knot   Knot   Knot   Leg Section

1"   ¼"   1"

Arm Section

BASIC INSTRUCTIONS:
Leg Section: Secure thread on the inside of a Yo Yo with a knot. Make a few stitches to anchor the thread. Run thread through a set of leg Yo Yos. Tie a knot close to the last Yo Yo. Skip 1" and tie another knot, skip ¼" and tie a knot, skip another 1" and tie a knot. Run thread through another set of leg Yo Yos. Make a few stitches to anchor the thread then make a knot inside of an end Yo Yo.
Arm Section: Repeat to make a shorter arm section.

Face Pattern

Face Pattern

Start Here

Body: Secure thread on the inside of a Yo Yo with a knot. Make a few stitches to anchor the thread. Run thread through the ¼" center in leg section, through a set of body Yo Yos, through the ¼" center in an arm section and through 1 Yo Yo at the neck. Make a few stitches to anchor the thread then make a knot inside of an end Yo Yo.

Green Hat for Clown

Cut 1 from this entire piece, do not split into hat and head.

Hat for Clowns with Pointed Hats

Cut 1

Head for Clowns with Pointed Hats

Cut 1

Cut here for Puppy and Sheep

Cut here for Giraffe and Spotted Dog

Tail for Animals (pages 18 - 19)

Cut 1

Cut here for Kitten and Tiger

Head: Cut out 2 head shapes. With right sides together, sew a ¼" seam around the shape (with small stitches). Clip the curves.

Secure thread on the inside of the neck Yo Yo with a knot. Make a few stitches to anchor the thread. Turn the edge under then stitch around the head, to attach it to the neck of body.
Optional Details:
Sew a small Pom Pom to each hand and foot.
Sew fabric strips to each hand and foot.
Embroider the eyes, nose and mouth.

Head for Clown with Green Hat

Cut 2

5½"

Head for Clown with Pink Ruffle

4½"

Sew a Tube

Back View

Face

Basic Instructions for a Neck Ruffle:

Cut a strip of fabric as specified.
Sew a ¼" hem along 1 long side.
Sew a gathering stitch along the other long side. Pull up thread to gather the ruffle around clown's neck. Tie a knot with the ends of thread then sew the ends of fabric together.

Basic Instructions for Face:

You'll need permanent marking pens or DMC floss (Red, Black, Blue) and a #22 chenille needle. Embroider or draw face.

Embellish:

Add rick rack, Pom Poms, etc. as desired.

Finish Doll:

Assemble the doll's body as shown on page 16.

Little Clown with Pink Ruffle - 9" tall

Fabric: 2¼ yds of assorted prints,
Muslin for the head, Pink for ruffle.
Ruffle: Cut a Pink strip of fabric 3½" x 25".
Yo Yos Make the following:
Cut 20 circles 5½"
(19 for body, 1 for hat)
Cut 76 circles 4¼"
(23 for each leg, 15 for each arm)
Head: Cut 1 head piece 4½" tall x 5½" across. Add the face. Sew the back seam. Gather at the top edge and bottom edge. Stuff with polyfil. Pull up thread to gather top and bottom of head. Tie a knot on each end. Sew a Yo Yo to the top of the head for a hat.

Clown with Green Hat - 9" tall

Fabric: 1½ yds of assorted prints,
Muslin for the head, Green for hat.
Ruffle: Cut a strip of tulle net 6" x 25".
TIP: Fold the strip in half to make ruffle.
Yo Yos - Make the following:
Cut 62 circles 4¼"
(10 for body, 14 for each leg,
12 for each arm)
Head: Cut 2 head pieces. Add the face. Sew pieces together. Stuff with polyfil. Gather at the neck edge and tie a secure knot.

Clowns with Pointed Hats - 9" tall

Fabric: 1⅝ yds of assorted prints.
Ruffles: Refer to individual clowns.
Cut a strip of Red fabric 4½" x 39".
Cut a strip of Black check 4½" x 25".
Pointed Hat and Head:
Cut a triangle for the hat.
Cut muslin for the head.
Sew the two hats and heads together.
Add the face.
Sew a back seam. Stuff with polyfil.
Gather fabric at the neck edge and tie a secure knot.
Yo Yos - Make the following::
Red Ruffle Clown:
Cut 18 circles 5½" for body
Cut 62 circles 4¼"
(18 for each leg, 13 for each arm)
Black Check Ruffle Clown:
Cut 14 circles 5½" for body
Cut 66 circles 4¼"
(19 for each leg, 14 for each arm)
Clown with Fabric Strips:
Cut 61 circles 5½" (13 for body,
13 for each leg, 11 for each arm)

Antique Yo Yo Dolls

Yo Yos have been made into quilts, clothing and dolls. These antique dolls features colorful arms and legs. They were made with love and have been carefully saved. Create your own Yo Yo dolls and clowns... they are fun to make and add color and cheer everywhere.

Yo Yo Animals

Create your own zoo with fabric stash leftovers. Creative critters are fun to make and share with family and friends.

Be sure to embroider the eyes instead of using buttons if the animal will be handled by a baby, toddler or child.

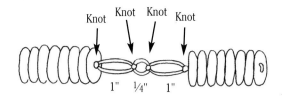

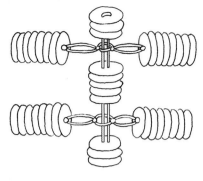

How to Assemble an Animal Body

BASIC SUPPLIES:
See patterns on pages 16 and 19.
Fabric as listed
DMC pearl cotton thread • Polyfil stuffing
• Thread and needle • #22 chenille needle
Optional: Yo Yo tools (Green, Orange, Yellow)
Optional: Two ½" buttons for eyes

Note: Use doubled thread throughout.

BASIC INSTRUCTIONS:
Leg Section:

Secure thread on the inside of a Yo Yo with a knot. Make a few stitches to anchor the thread. Run thread through a set of leg Yo Yos. Tie a knot close to the last Yo Yo. Skip 1" and tie another knot, skip ¼" and tie a knot, skip another 1" and tie a knot. Run thread through another set of leg Yo Yos. Make a few stitches to anchor the thread then make a knot inside of an end Yo Yo.

Repeat to make another leg section.

Body:

Secure thread on the inside of a Yo Yo with a knot. Make a few stitches to anchor the thread. Run thread through 3 Yo Yos, through the ¼" center in a leg section, through a set of body Yo Yos, through the ¼" center in a leg section and through 3 Yo Yos. Make a few stitches to anchor the thread then make a knot inside of an end Yo Yo.

Large
Head
Pattern i
for
Tiger
(page 18

Cut 2

Small
Head
Pattern
is for
Puppy
Sheep
and Kitt
(page 19

Cut 2